A NOTE TO PARENTS ABOUT SHOWING OFF

Showing off seldom produces the kind of attention that show-offs seek. There are better ways to be noticed and accepted.

The purpose of this book is to teach children that it is unnecessary for anyone to prove that he or she is superior to others. Positive attributes that deserve to be noticed will garner attention on their own.

Taking pride in one's personal characteristics or accomplishments should never be considered showing off. Neither should performing in acceptable arenas. Children should feel good enough about themselves to seek, in appropriate ways, the attention they deserve and need. They should also be taught how to accept and be thankful for well-deserved praise and attention.

By reading and discussing this book with your child, you can encourage him or her to seek attention in appropriate ways. You can also affirm your child's self-esteem so he or she will not be intimidated by show-offs.

A Children's Book About

SHOWING OFF

Managing Editor: Ellen Klarberg
Copy Editor: Annette Gooch
Editorial Assistant: Lana Eberhard
Art Director: Jennifer Wiezel
Production Artist: Gail Miller
Illustration Designer: Bartholomew
Inking Artist: Rashida Tessler
Coloring Artist: Linda Hanney
Lettering Artist: Linda Hanney
Typographer: Communication Graphics

A Children's Book About

SHOWING OFF

By Joy Berry

GROLIER
B O O K S

GROLIER BOOKS IS A DIVISION OF GROLIER ENTERPRISES, INC.

This book is about Toni and her friends Annie and Sam.

Reading about Toni and her friends can help you understand and deal with **showing off.**

Have you ever been with people who try to make you think they are better than you?

People are showing off when they do things to make you think they are better than you are.

When you are with someone who is showing off:

- How do you feel?
- What do you think?
- What do you do?

When you are with someone who is showing off:

- You might feel unimportant.
- You might feel as if you cannot do anything well.
- You might decide you do not want to be with a person who makes you feel bad about yourself.

It is important to treat others the way you want to be treated.

If you do not want other people to show off, you must not show off.

There are many ways to show off.

Some people show off by *saying they are better than others.* This is called bragging.

There are many things people try to prove by showing off.

Some people show off to try to prove they are *more important than others.*

These people do not understand that no one person is more important than anyone else.

We are each important in our own way.

Some people show off to try to prove *they can do things better than others.*

These people do not understand that no one person can be the best at doing everything.

Some people are good at doing some things. Other people are good at doing other things.

Every person can do something well.

Some people show off to try to prove they are *smarter than others.*

These people do not understand that no one person can be smarter than everyone else.

Some of us know some things. Others know other things.

We are each smart in our own way.

Some people show off to try to prove they *have more than others.*

These people do not understand that having things does not make a person important.

People are important because of what they are, not because of what they have.

Some people show off to try to prove they *are more popular than others.* (Being popular means being well known.)

These people do not understand that people can be well known for the wrong reasons. Some people are well known because they do bad things.

It is more important to be a person who does good things than it is to be a person who is well known.

You will be happiest when you treat others the way you want to be treated.

This means you will not show off because you do not like it when others show off.